Easy Guitar with Tab

The Rolling Stones

EASY GUITAR COLLECTION

Cover Photo by David Lefranc / Getty Images

ISBN 978-1-4950-7687-9

7777 W. BLUEMOUND RD. P.O. BOX 13819 MILWAUKEE, WI 53213

In Australia Contact:
Hal Leonard Australia Pty. Ltd.
4 Lentara Court
Cheltenham, Victoria, 3192 Australia
Email: ausadmin@halleonard.com.au

Visit Hal Leonard Online at
www.halleonard.com

STRUM AND PICK PATTERNS

This chart contains the suggested strum and pick patterns that are referred to by number at the beginning of each song in this book. The symbols ⊓ and ∨ in the strum patterns refer to down and up strokes, respectively. The letters in the pick patterns indicate which right-hand fingers play which strings.

p = thumb
i = index finger
m = middle finger
a = ring finger

For example; Pick Pattern 2
is played: thumb - index - middle - ring

Strum Patterns   Pick Patterns

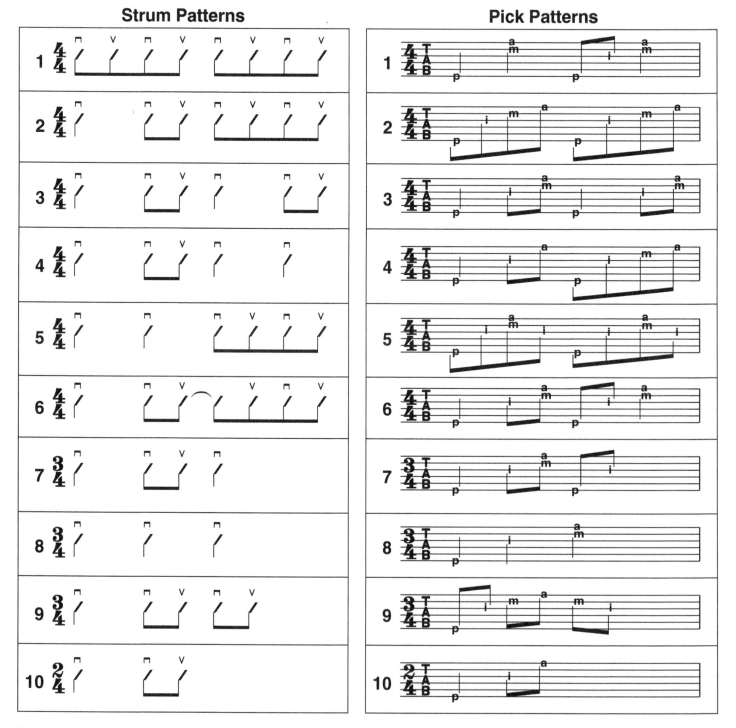

You can use the 3/4 Strum and Pick Patterns in songs written in compound meter (6/8, 9/8, 12/8, etc.).
For example, you can accompany a song in 6/8 by playing the 3/4 pattern twice in each measure.
The 4/4 Strum and Pick Patterns can be used for songs written in cut time (¢) by doubling the note time values in the patterns. Each pattern would therefore last two measures in cut time.

Doo Doo Doo Doo Doo
(Heartbreaker)

Words and Music by Mick Jagger and Keith Richards

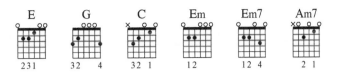

Strum Pattern: 5, 6
Pick Pattern: 1

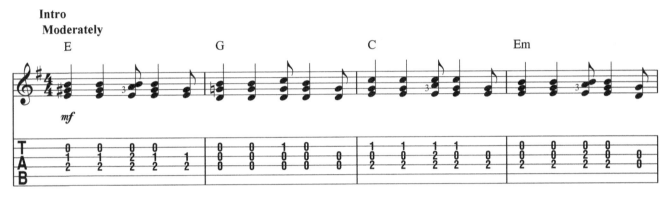

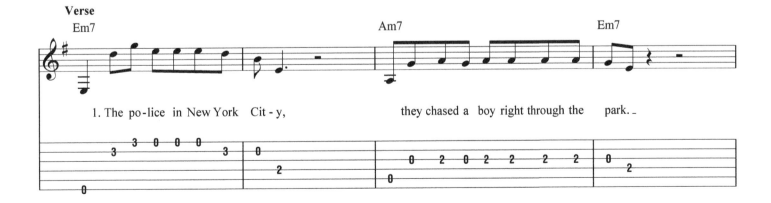

Angie

Words and Music by Mick Jagger and Keith Richards

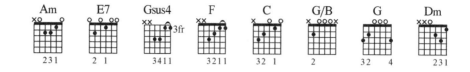

Strum Pattern: 1
Pick Pattern: 5

1. An - gie, An - gie,
2. *See additional lyrics*
3. *Instrumental*

when will those clouds all dis - ap - pear? _____ An - gie, _____

An - gie, where will it lead us from here? _____ 1. With no

Verse

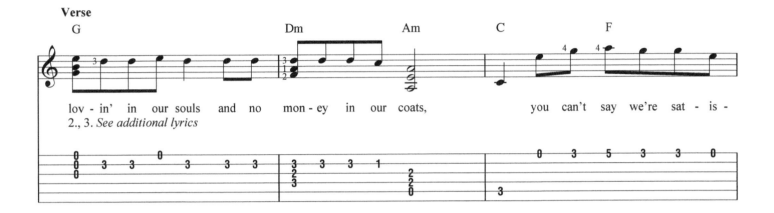

lov - in' in our souls and no mon - ey in our coats, you can't say we're sat - is -
2., 3. *See additional lyrics*

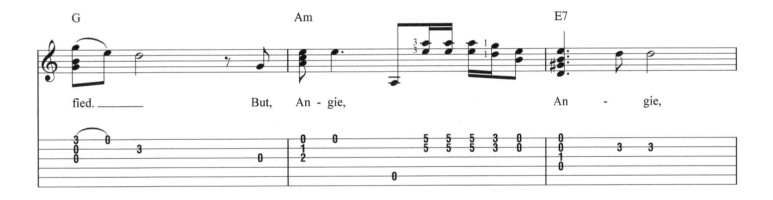

fied. _____ But, An - gie, An - gie,

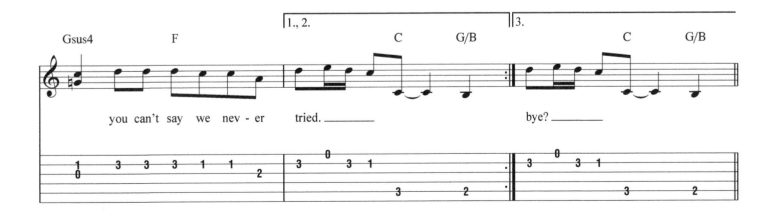

you can't say we nev - er tried. _____ bye? _____

Interlude

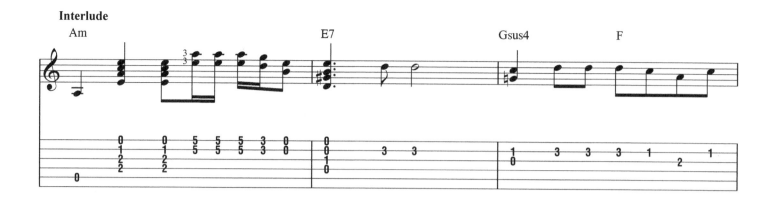

Verse

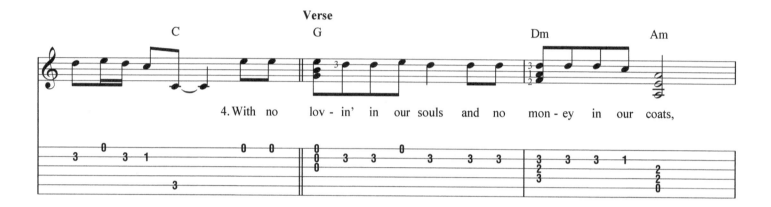

4. With no lov - in' in our souls and no mon - ey in our coats,

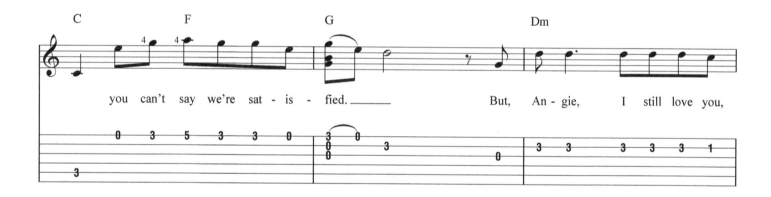

you can't say we're sat - is - fied. _____ But, An - gie, I still love you,

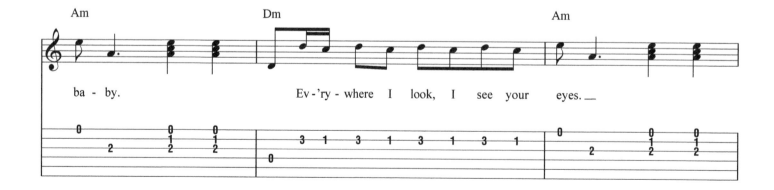

ba - by. Ev - 'ry - where I look, I see your eyes. __

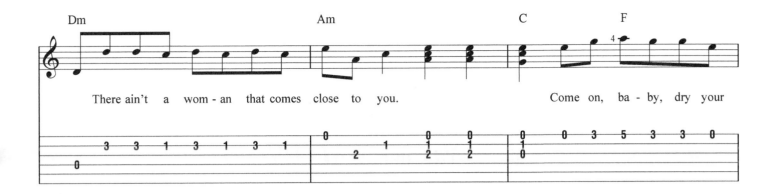

Outro-Chorus

Additional Lyrics

Chorus 2: Angie, you're beautiful,
But ain't it time we said goodbye?
Angie, I still love you.
Remember all those nights we cried.

2. All the dreams we held so close
Seemed to all go up in smoke.
Let me whisper in your ear,
Angie, Angie,
Where will it lead us from here?

3. Oh, Angie, don't you weep,
Oh, your kisses still taste sweet.
I hate that sadness in your eyes.
But Angie, Angie,
Ain't it time we said goodbye?

Beast of Burden

Words and Music by Mick Jagger and Keith Richards

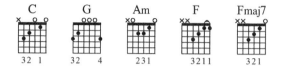

*Capo IV

Strum Pattern: 2, 4
Pick Pattern: 5, 6

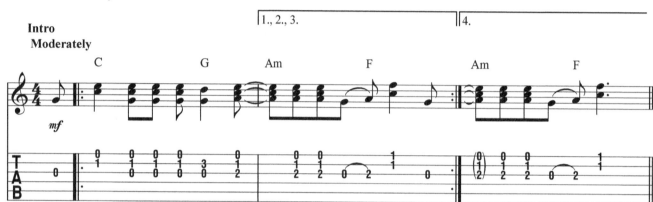

*Optional: To match recording, place capo at 4th fret.

1. I'll nev - er be ___ your beast of bur - den.   My back is broad, ___ but it's a hurt - in'.
4. *See additional lyrics*

All I want is for you to make love to me. ___

Verse

2. I'll nev-er be ___ your beast of bur - den. I've walked for miles; ___ my feet are hurt-in'.
3., 5. *See additional lyrics*

To Coda ⊕

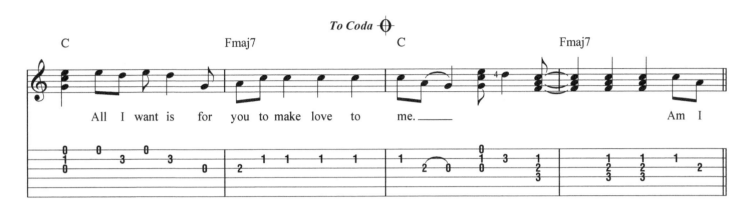

All I want is for you to make love to me. ___ Am I

Chorus

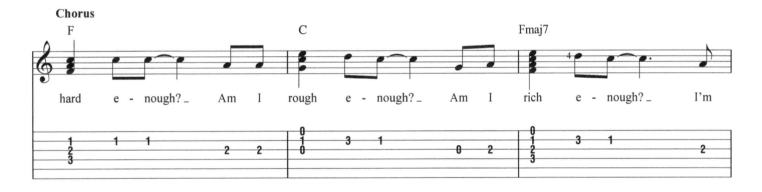

hard e - nough? ___ Am I rough e - nough? ___ Am I rich e - nough? ___ I'm

1. | **2.**

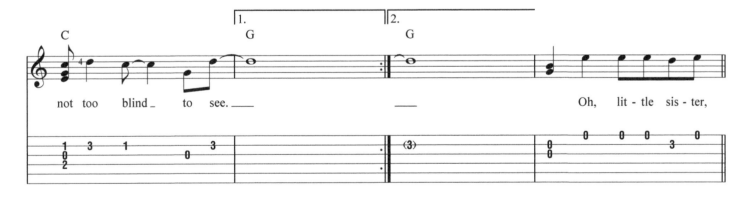

not too blind ___ to see. ___ Oh, lit - tle sis - ter,

1., 2.

Guitar Solo

pret - ty, pret - ty, pret - ty, pret - ty girls. ___

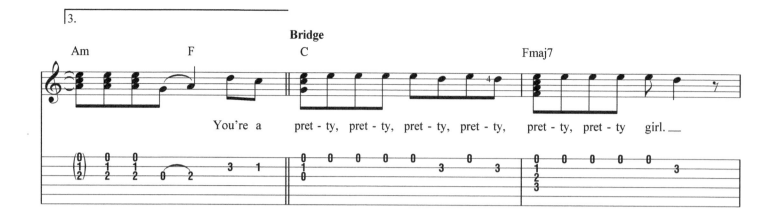

You're a pret - ty, pret - ty, pret - ty, pret - ty, pret - ty, pret - ty girl. __

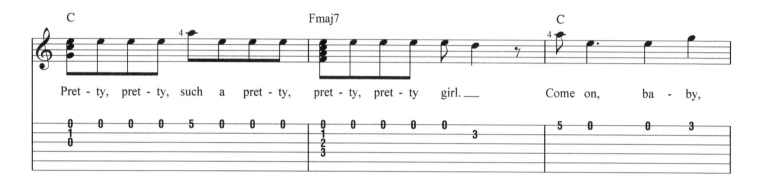

Pret - ty, pret - ty, such a pret - ty, pret - ty, pret - ty girl. __ Come on, ba - by,

D.S. al Coda

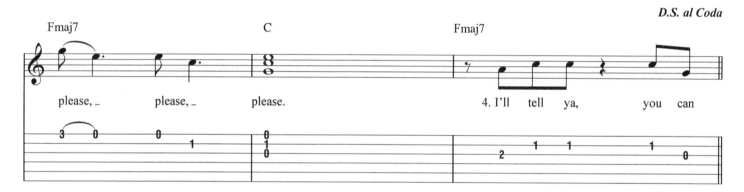

please, __ please, __ please. 4. I'll tell ya, you can

Coda

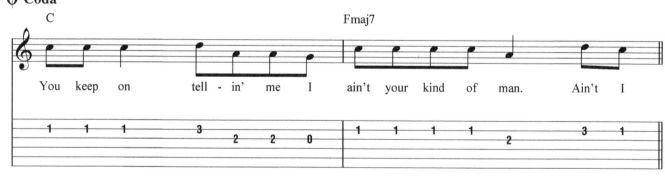

You keep on tell - in' me I ain't your kind of man. Ain't I

Chorus

rough e - nough? Oo, hon - ey. Ain't I tough e - nough? Ain't I

Additional Lyrics

3. I'll never be your beast of burden.
So let's go home and draw the curtains.
Music on the radio; come on, baby, make sweet love to me.

4. I'll tell ya, you can put me out on the street.
Put me out with no shoes on my feet.
But put me out, put me out, put me out of misery.

5. All the sickness, I can suck it up.
Throw it all at me, I can shrug it off.
There's one thing, baby, I don't understand.
You keep on tellin' me I ain't your kind of man.

7. I'll never be your beast of burden.
I've walked for miles; my feet are hurtin'.
All I want is you to make love to me.

8. I don't need no beast of burden.
I need no fussin', I need no nursin'.
Never, never, never, never, never, never, never need.

Emotional Rescue

Words and Music by Mick Jagger and Keith Richards

*Capo III

Strum Pattern: 1
Pick Pattern: 5

Intro
Moderately

*Optional: To match recording, place capo at 3rd fret.

Verse

1. Is there noth-in' I could say, noth-in' I could do change your mind? I'm
4. *See additional lyrics*

so in love with you. Too deep-ly you're kind-a out,___

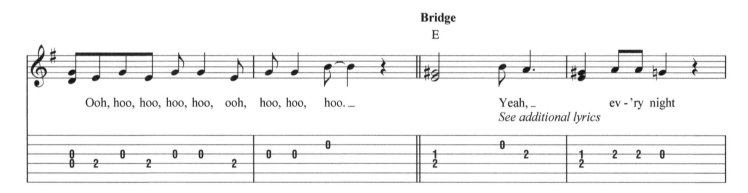

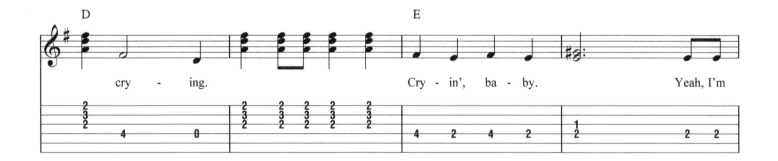

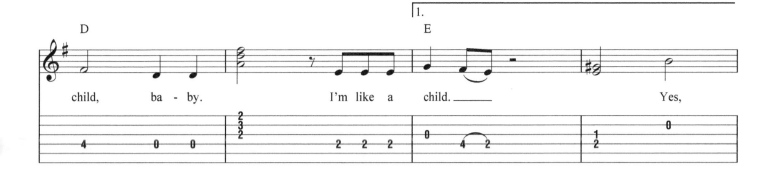

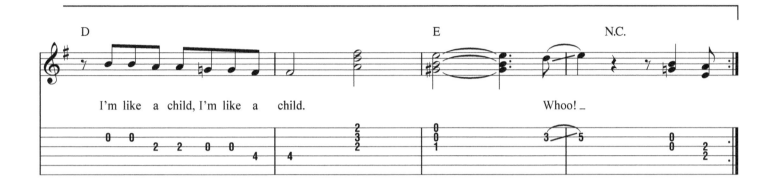

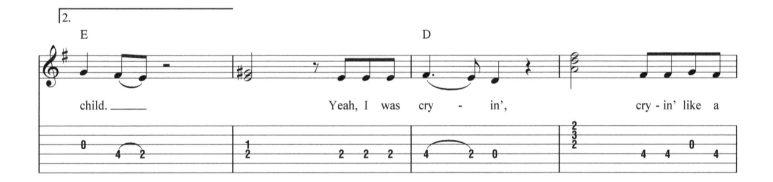

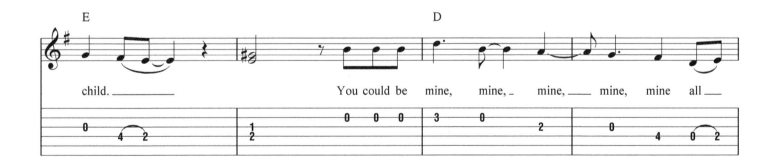

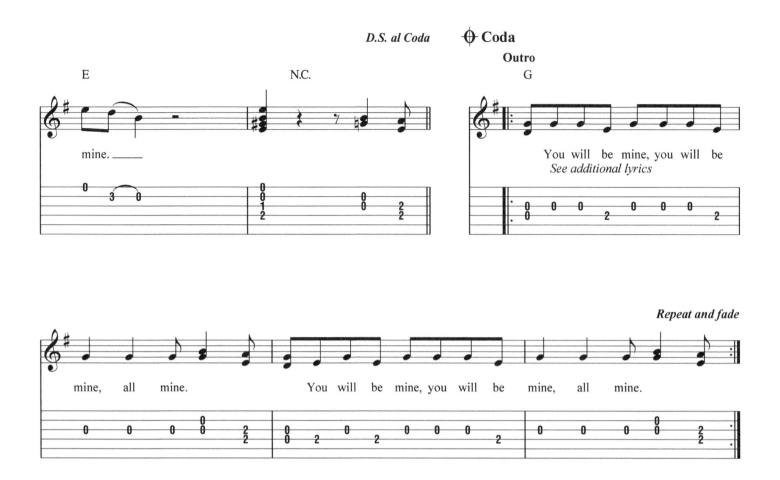

Additional Lyrics

3. You think you're one of a special breed.
   You think that you're his pet Pekinese.
   I'll be your savior, steadfast and true.
   I'll come to your emotional rescue.
   I'll come to your emotional rescue.

Chorus 3: Ooh, ah, ah, ah, ah, ah, ah, ah.
   Ah, ah, ah, ah, ah, ah, ah, ah.

Bridge: Yeah, I was dreamin' last night, baby.
   Last night I was dreamin' that you'd be mine.
   But I was cryin' like a child.
   Yeah, I was cryin', cryin' like a child.
   You could be mine, mine, mine, mine, mine all mine.
   You could be mine, could be mine, could be mine all mine.

4. I come to you, so silent in the night,
   So stealthy, so animal quiet.
   I'll be your savior, steadfast and true.
   I'll come to your emotional rescue.
   I'll come to your emotional rescue.

Chorus 4: Ah, ah, ah, ah, ah, ah, ah, ah.
   Yeah, you should be mine, mine, ooh!

5. *Spoken: Mmm, yes, you could be mine, tonight and every night.*
   I will be your knight in shining armor
   Coming to your emotional rescue.

Outro: Spoken: I will be your knight in shining armor
   Riding across the desert on a fine Arab charger.

Happy

Words and Music by Mick Jagger and Keith Richards

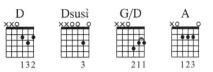

*Capo II

Strum Pattern: 5
Pick Pattern: 6

Intro
Moderately fast

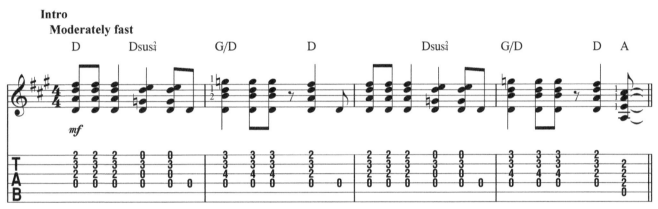

*Optional: To match recording, place capo at 2nd fret.

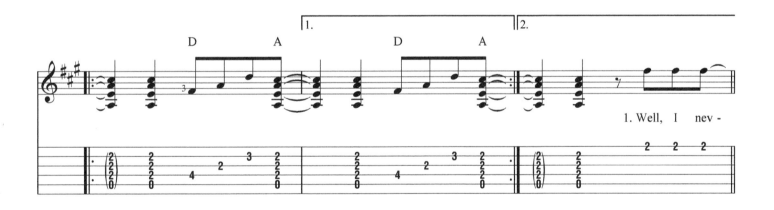

1. Well, I nev-

Verse

-er kept a dol-lar past sun-set, al-ways burned a hole in my pants.
2., 3. See additional lyrics

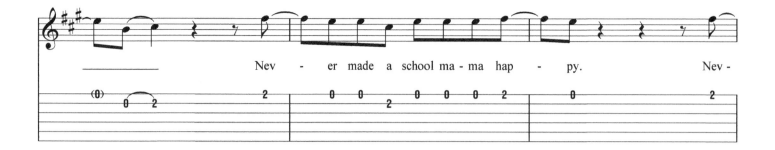

Nev - er made a school ma - ma hap - py. Nev -

Chorus

- er blew a sec - ond chance __ on love. __ I need a love __ to

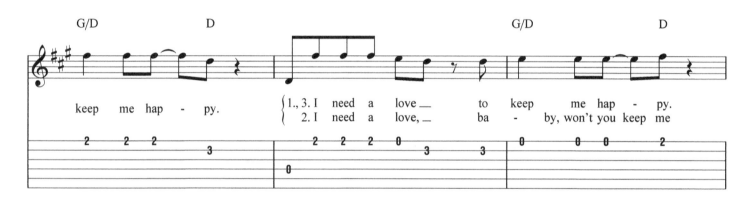

keep me hap - py.
1., 3. I need a love __ to keep me hap - py.
2. I need a love, __ ba - by, won't you keep me

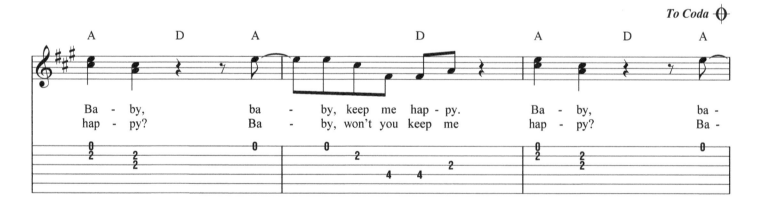

To Coda ⊕

Ba - by, ba - by, keep me hap - py. Ba - by, ba - by,
hap - py? Ba - by, won't you keep me hap - py? Ba -

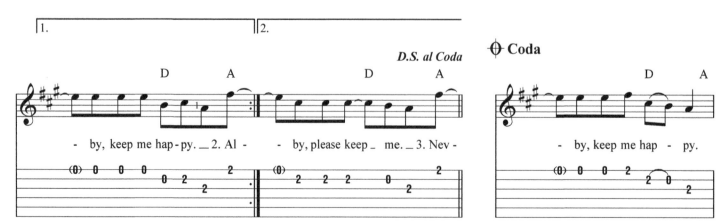

D.S. al Coda ⊕ **Coda**

- by, keep me hap - py. __ 2. Al - by, please keep __ me. __ 3. Nev - by, keep me hap - py.

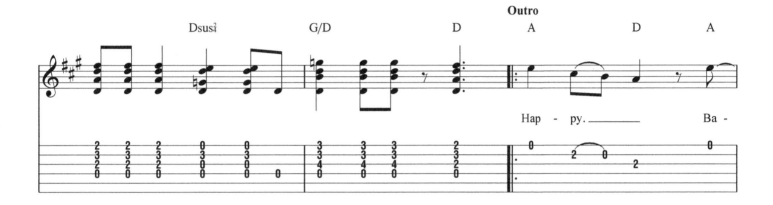

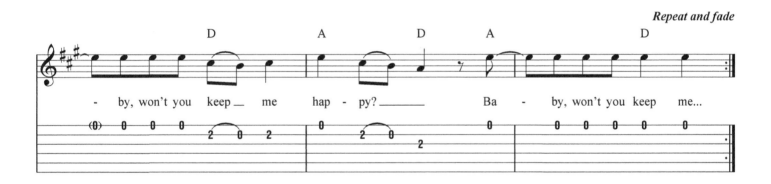

Additional Lyrics

2. Always took candy from strangers,
   Didn't wanna get me no trade.
   Never want to be like Papa;
   Workin' for the boss ev'ry night and day.

3. Never got a flash out of cocktails
   When I got some flesh off the bone.
   Never got a lift out of Lear jet
   When I can fly way back home.

Fool to Cry

Words and Music by Mick Jagger and Keith Richards

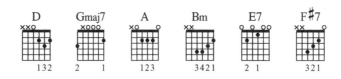

*Capo III

Strum Pattern: 2
Pick Pattern: 2

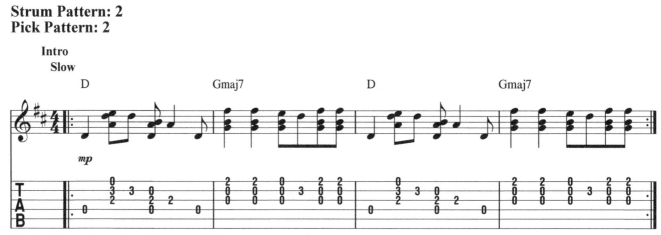

*Optional: To match recording, place capo at 3rd fret.

1. When I come home, ba-by, and I've been work-ing all night long,
2. *See additional lyrics*

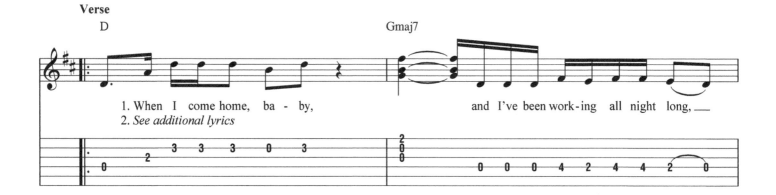

put my daugh-ter on my knee and she say,

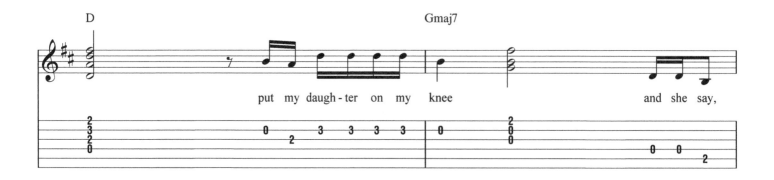

"Dad - dy, what's wrong?" ___

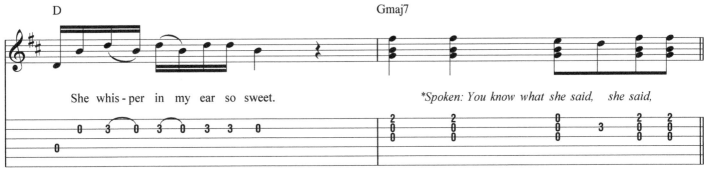

She whis - per in my ear so sweet. *Spoken: You know what she said, she said,*

*Lyrics in italics are spoken throughout.

Chorus

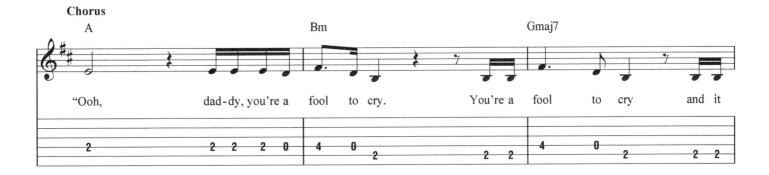

"Ooh, dad - dy, you're a fool to cry. You're a fool to cry and it

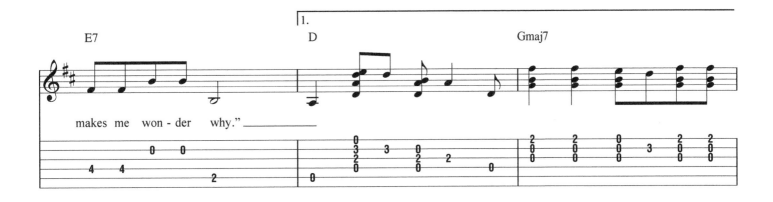

makes me won - der why." _____

Dad - dy, you're a fool. _____ *2. You know,* Ooh, dad - dy, you're a

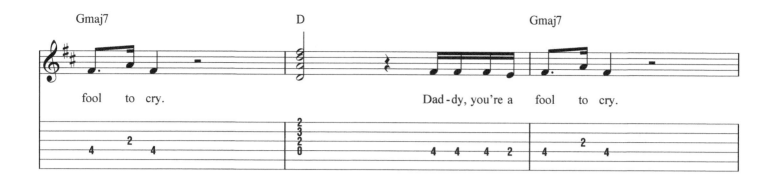

fool to cry. Dad-dy, you're a fool to cry.

Dad-dy, you're a fool to cry. *Yeah, she said,*

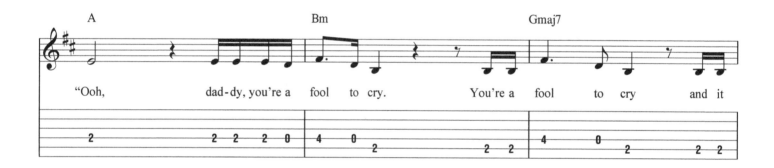

"Ooh, dad-dy, you're a fool to cry. You're a fool to cry and it

A tempo

makes me won-der why." *She said,* "Ooh, ooh, dad-dy, you're a fool to cry." _____

Even my friends say to me sometime, I'm think, I like, I don't understand.

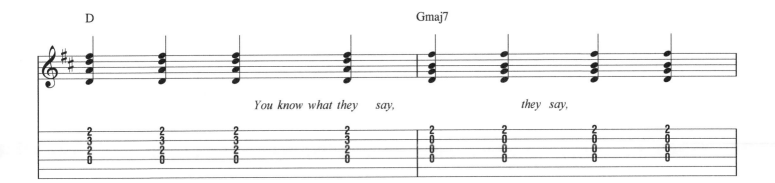

You know what they say, they say,

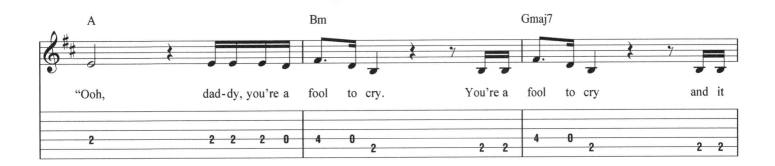

"Ooh, dad-dy, you're a fool to cry. You're a fool to cry and it

Outro

w/ Voc. ad lib.

Repeat and fade

makes me won - der why."

Additional Lyrics

2. You know, I got a woman
   And she lives in the poor part of town.
   And I go see her sometimes
   And we make love, so fine.
   I put my head on her shoulder.
   She says, "Tell me all your troubles."
   You know what she says?
   She says,...

It's Only Rock 'N' Roll (But I Like It)

Words and Music by Mick Jagger and Keith Richards

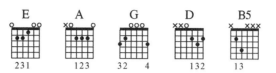

Strum Pattern: 2, 4
Pick Pattern: 3, 4

Intro
Moderately fast

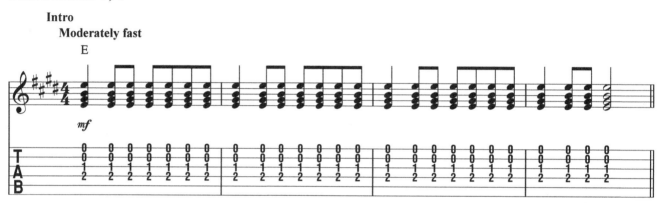

Verse

1. If I could stick __ my pen __ in my heart, __ I would spill it all o - ver the stage.
2. If I could stick __ a knife __ in my heart, __ su - i - cide right on the stage,

__ Would __ it sat - is - fy ya, would __ it slide on by ya, would __
__ would __ it be e - nough for your __ teen - age lust, would __

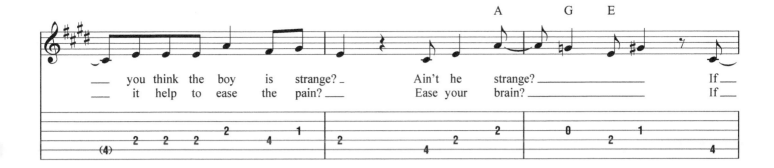

you think the boy is strange? ___ Ain't he strange? _____ If ___
it help to ease the pain? ___ Ease your brain? _____ If ___

___ I could win __ ya, if ___ I could sing __ ya a love song so di - vine. __
___ I could dig __ down deep ___ in my heart, ___ feel-ings would flood on the page. __

3. *Instrumental*

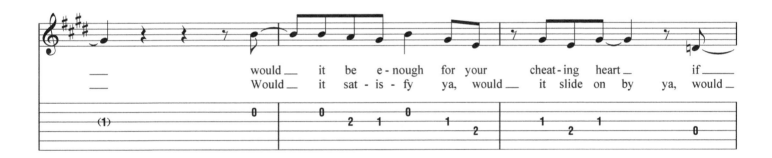

___ would ___ it be e - nough for your cheat-ing heart ___ if _____
___ Would ___ it sat - is - fy ya, would ___ it slide on by ya, would ___

To Coda

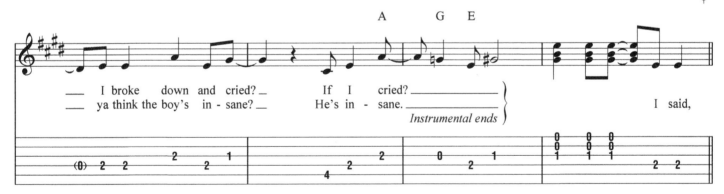

___ I broke down and cried? __ If I cried? _____
___ ya think the boy's in - sane? __ He's in - sane. _____

Instrumental ends

I said,

Chorus

"I know ___ it's on - ly rock 'n' roll ___ but I like it. _____

I know — it's on-ly rock 'n' roll — but I

like it, like it, yes, I do." — Oh, well, I like it,   I

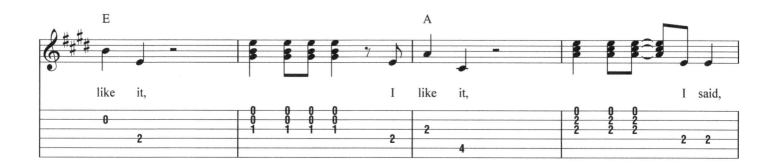

like it,   I like it,   I said,

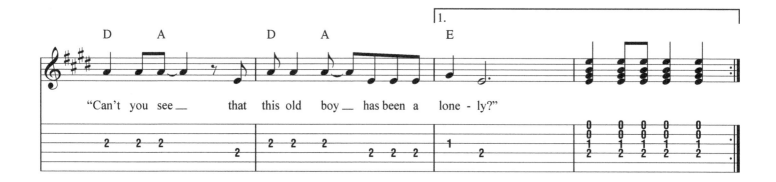

1.

"Can't you see — that this old boy — has been a lone - ly?"

2.

Bridge

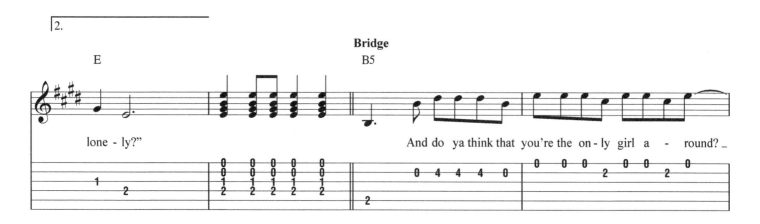

lone - ly?"   And do ya think that you're the on-ly girl a - round? —

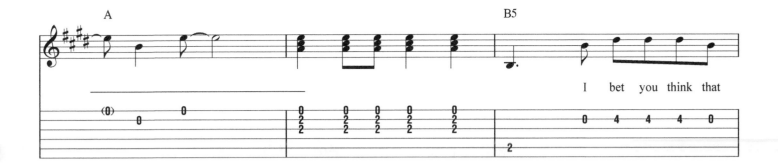

I bet you think that

D.S. al Coda

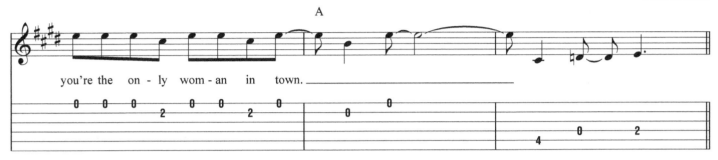

you're the on - ly wom - an in town. ____

⊕ **Coda**

Chorus

Play 3 times

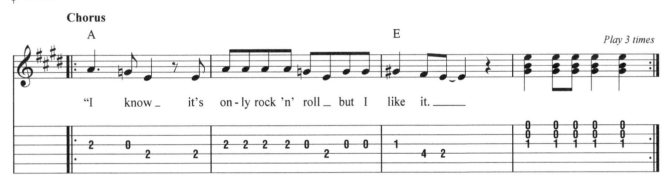

"I know ___ it's on - ly rock 'n' roll ___ but I like it. ____

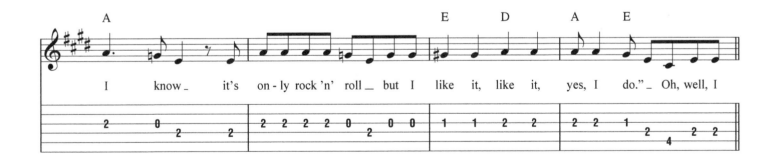

I know ___ it's on - ly rock 'n' roll ___ but I like it, like it, yes, I do." ___ Oh, well, I

Outro

Repeat and fade

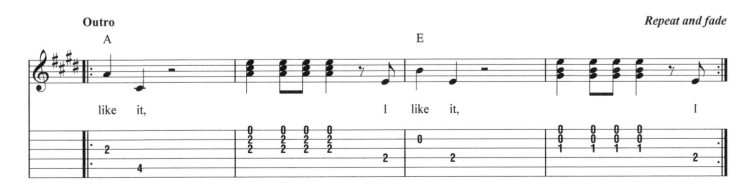

like it, I like it, I

Miss You

Words and Music by Mick Jagger and Keith Richards

Strum Pattern: 3
Pick Pattern: 4

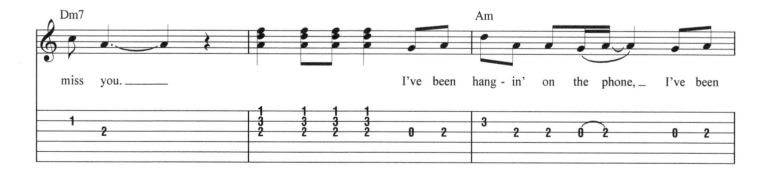

sleep-in' all a-lone.___ I wan-na kiss you _____ *sometime.* Oo, ___

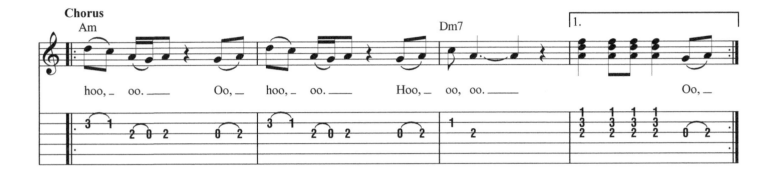

Chorus

hoo, _ oo. ___ Oo, _ hoo, _ oo. ___ Hoo, _ oo, oo. _____ Oo, _

Verse

2. Well, I've been haunt-ed in my sleep, _ you've been star - in' in my dreams. _ Lord, I

miss you, child. ___ I've been wait - in' in the hall, _ been

wait - in' on your call, when the phone rings._____ *Spoken: It's just some friends of mine. They say, "Hey!*

What's the matter man? We're gonna come 'round at twelve with some Puerto Rican girls that's just dy'n' to meet you! We're gonna

bring a case of wine.   Hey, let's go mess and fool around, you know, like we used to!"   Ah, —

|1.

Chorus

ah, — ah. ___   Ah, — ah, — ah. ___   Ah, — ah, ah. ___   Ah, —

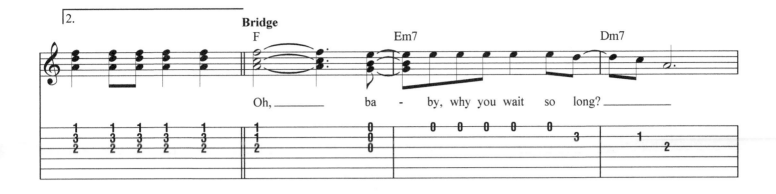

Oh, _____ ba - by, why you wait so long? _____

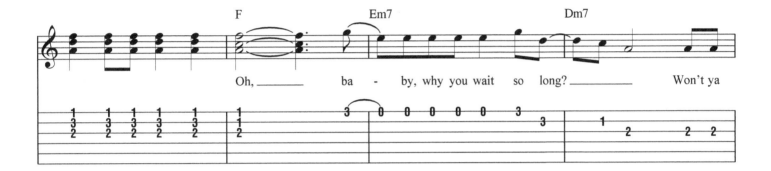

Oh, _____ ba - by, why you wait so long? _____ Won't ya

come home? Come home!

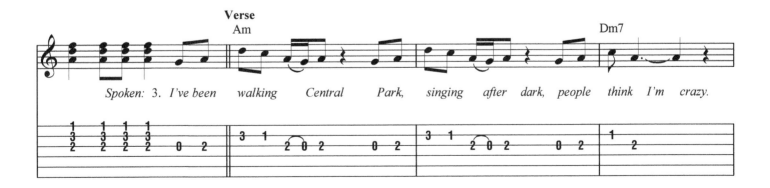

Spoken: 3. *I've been walking Central Park, singing after dark, people think I'm crazy.*

Stumbling on my feet, shuffling through the street, asking me,

"What's the matter with you, boy?" Sometimes what I wanna say to myself...

Chorus

Sometimes I say... 1. Oo, _ (2.) hoo, _ oo. _ Oo, _ hoo, _ oo. _ Oo, _ oo. _
3., 4. *Instrumental*

Verse

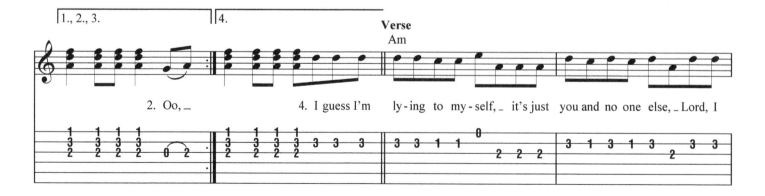

2. Oo, _ 4. I guess I'm ly-ing to my-self, _ it's just you and no one else, _ Lord, I

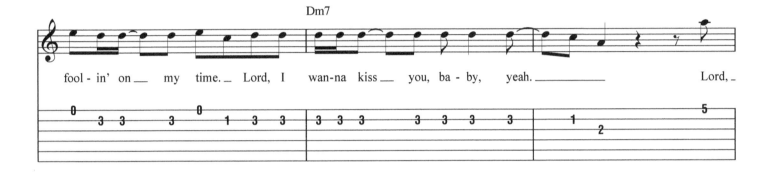

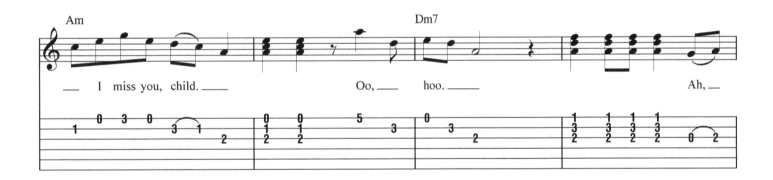

Outro-Chorus

Repeat and fade

One Hit (To the Body)

Words and Music by Mick Jagger, Keith Richards and Ronnie Wood

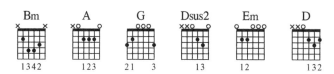

Strum Pattern: 6
Pick Pattern: 1

Intro
  Moderately fast

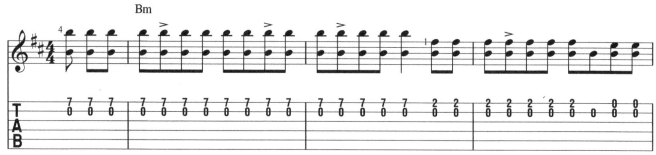

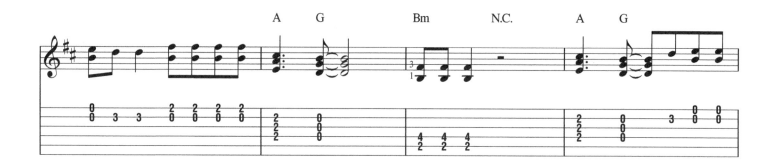

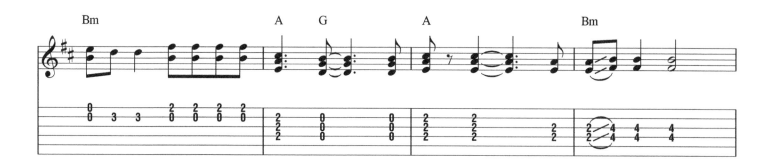

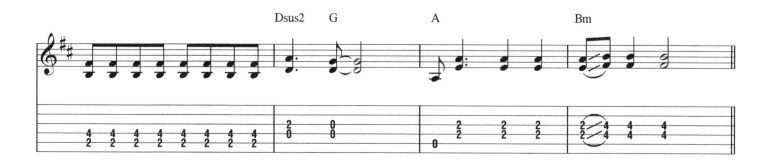

Verse

1. You fell out of the clear ___ blue sky ___ to the dark - ness be - low. ___
2., 4. *See additional lyrics*

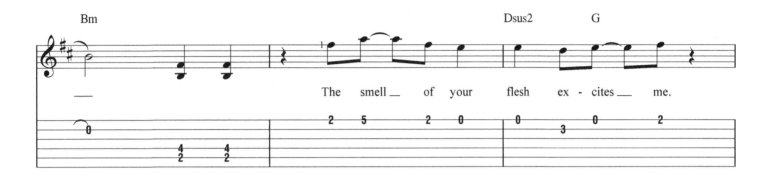

___ The smell ___ of your flesh ex - cites ___ me.

My blood ___ starts to flow, ___ so help me, God.

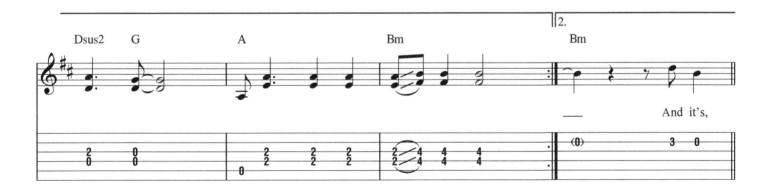

___ And it's,

Chorus

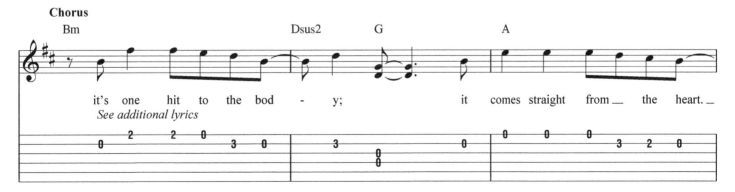

it's one hit to the bod - y; it comes straight from ___ the heart. ___
See additional lyrics

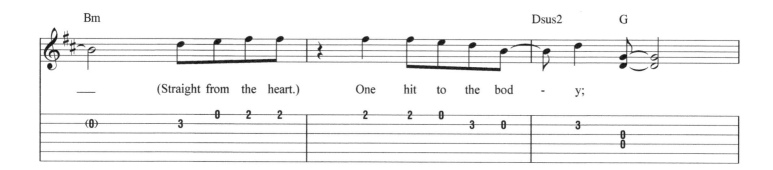

To Coda ⊕

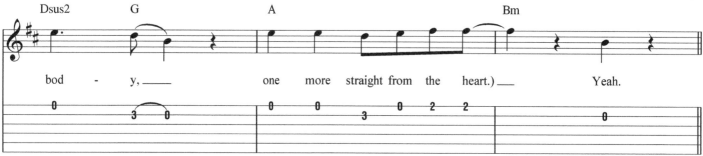

Verse

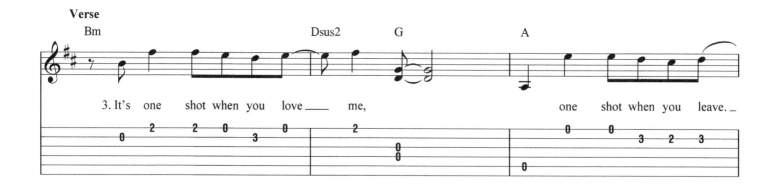

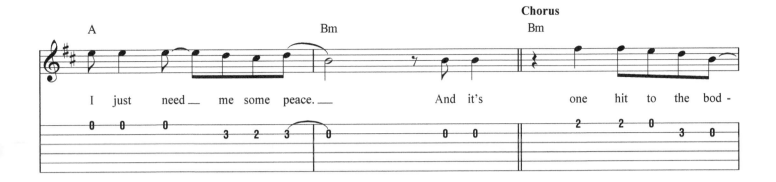

I just need ___ me some peace. ___ And it's one hit to the bod -

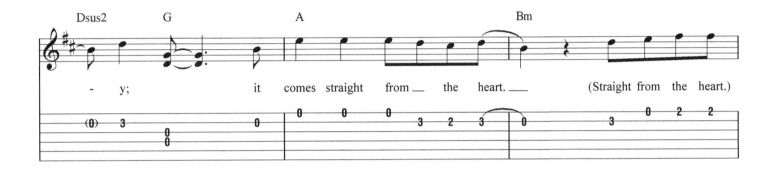

- y; it comes straight from ___ the heart. ___ (Straight from the heart.)

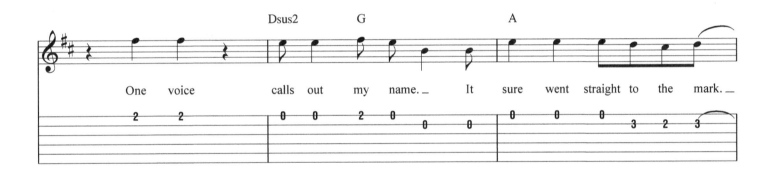

One voice calls out my name. ___ It sure went straight to the mark. ___

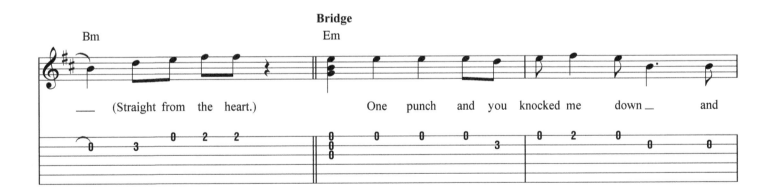

___ (Straight from the heart.) One punch and you knocked me down ___ and

tore my de - fens - es a - part. ___ One round took me

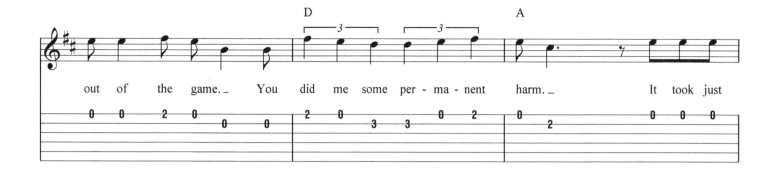

out of the game. _ You did me some per - ma - nent harm. _ It took just

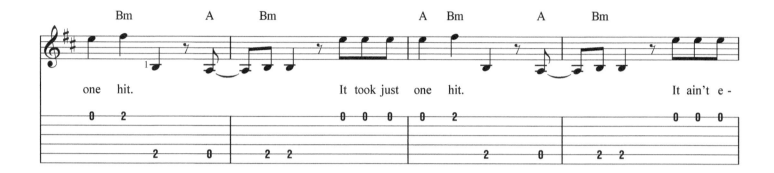

one hit. It took just one hit. It ain't e -

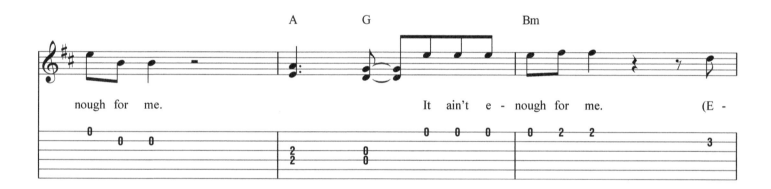

nough for me. It ain't e - nough for me. (E -

nough for me.) It ain't e - nough for me and I can't keep fight - ing, hey! _

Guitar Solo

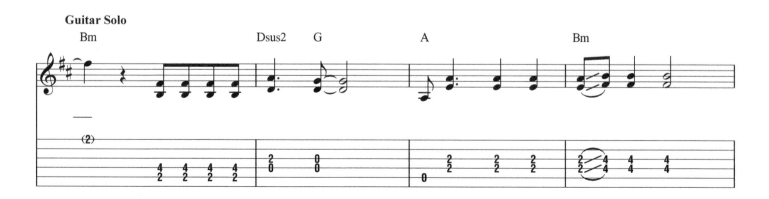

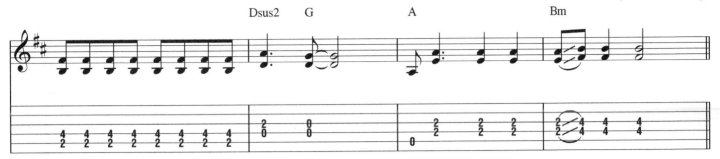

⊕ Coda

Outro

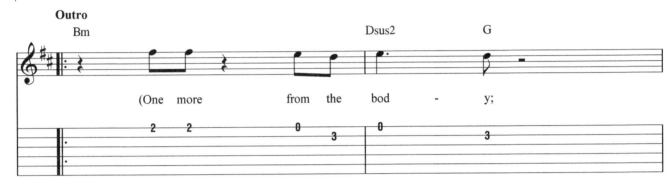

(One more   from   the   bod -   y;

Repeat and fade

one   more   straight from   the   heart, _____   straight from   the   heart.)

Additional Lyrics

2. You burst in, in a blaze of light;
   You unzipper the dark.
   One kiss took my breath away,
   One look lights up the stars.

4. Oh, your love is just a sweet addiction;
   I can't clean you out of my veins.
   It's a lifelong affliction
   That has damaged my brain.

Chorus It took just one hit to the body to tear my defenses apart.
   (Straight from the heart.)
   One hit to the body; it sure went straight to the mark.
   (Straight from the heart.)
   One hit to the body that comes straight from the heart.
   (Straight from the heart.)

Rock and a Hard Place

Words and Music by Mick Jagger and Keith Richards

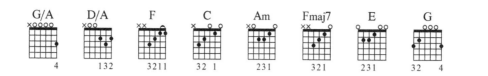

Strum Pattern: 2
Pick Pattern: 4

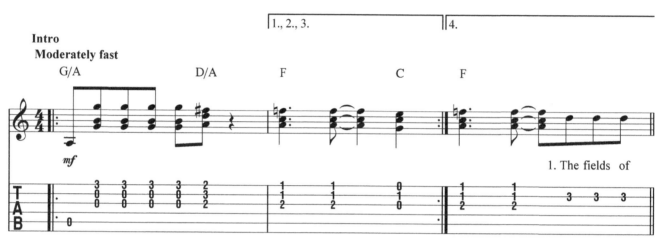

1. The fields of

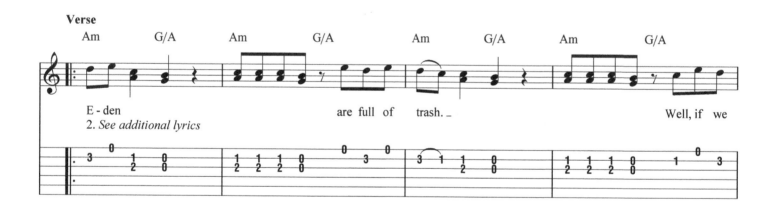

E - den
2. *See additional lyrics*

are full of trash. __

Well, if we

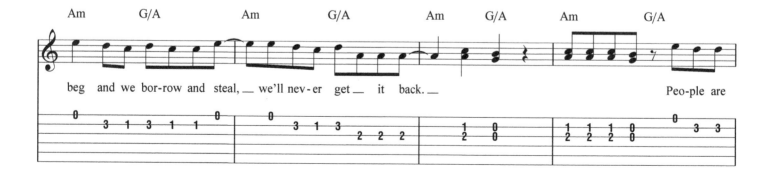

beg and we bor-row and steal, __ we'll nev-er get __ it back. __

Peo-ple are

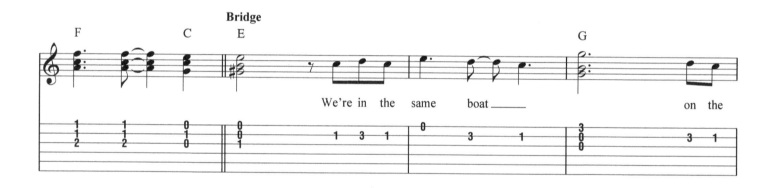

sil - ver spires. _____ And our own chil - dren are play - ing

Guitar Solo

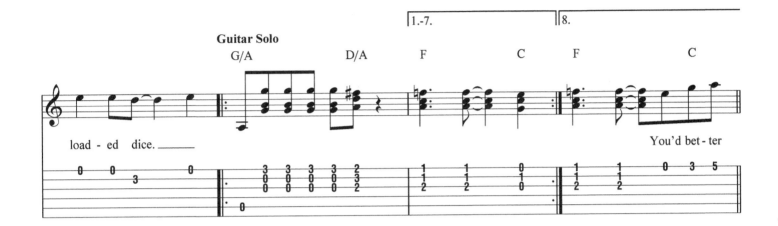

load - ed dice. _____ You'd bet - ter

Interlude

stop! Give me the truth, now. _____ Don't want no

sham. _____ I'd be hung, drawn and quar - tered for a sheep just as well as a

lamb. Stuck be - tween a rock and a hard place, _ a

rock   and a hard   place. _ You'd bet-ter stop,   put on a kind face. _____

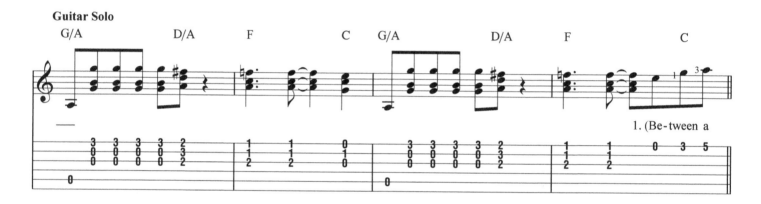

Ooh, yeah,   can't you see _____   what you've done to me? _____

Guitar Solo

1. (Be-tween a

Chorus

| 1., 2. |

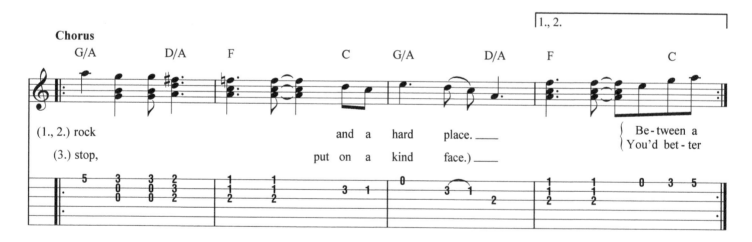

(1., 2.) rock   and a hard   place. _____   { Be-tween a
(3.) stop,   put on a kind face.) _____   { You'd bet - ter

| 3. |

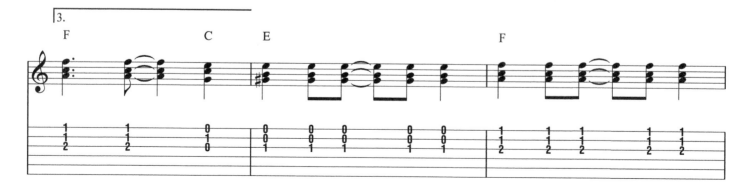

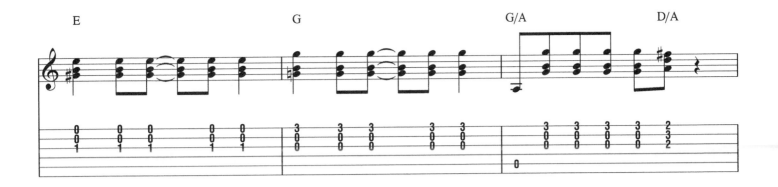

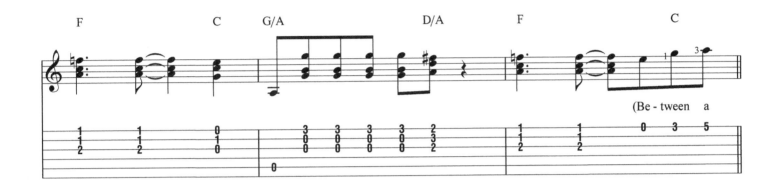

(Be - tween a

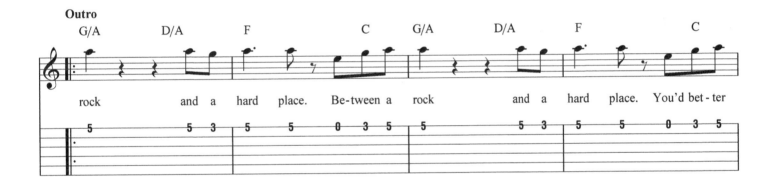

rock　　　　and a　hard　place.　Be-tween a　rock　　　and a　hard　place.　You'd bet - ter

Repeat and fade

stop,　　　put on a　kind　face.　You'd bet - ter　stop,　　　put on a　kind　face.)　(Be-tween a

Additional Lyrics

2. This talk of freedom and human rights,
   Means bullying and private wars and chucking all the dust into our eyes.
   And peasant people, poorer than dirt,
   Who are caught in the crossfire and got nothin' to lose but their shirts.

Rocks Off

Words and Music by Mick Jagger and Keith Richards

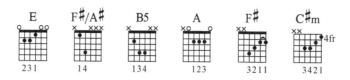

Strum Pattern: 2
Pick Pattern: 6

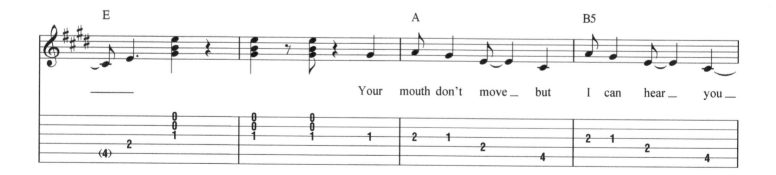

𝄋 Verse

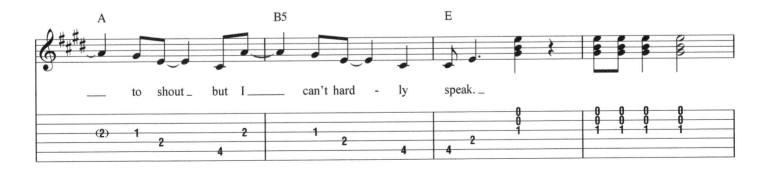

I was mak-in' love last night ____ to a danc-er friend of mine. ____

I can't seem to stay in step _'cause she comes _ ev-'ry time _ that she pir - ou-ettes _ o-ver me. _

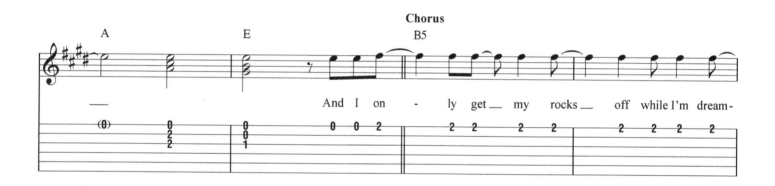

And I on - ly get _ my rocks _ off while I'm dream-

- ing. I on - ly get _ my rocks _ off while I'm sleep-

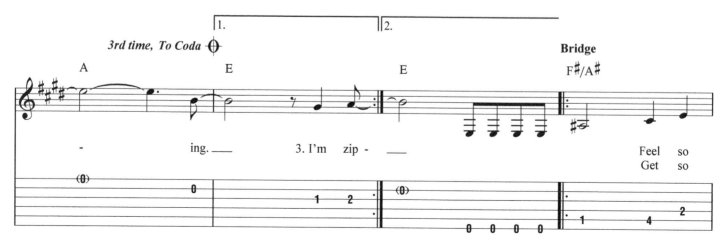

- ing. ____ 3. I'm zip - Feel so / Get so

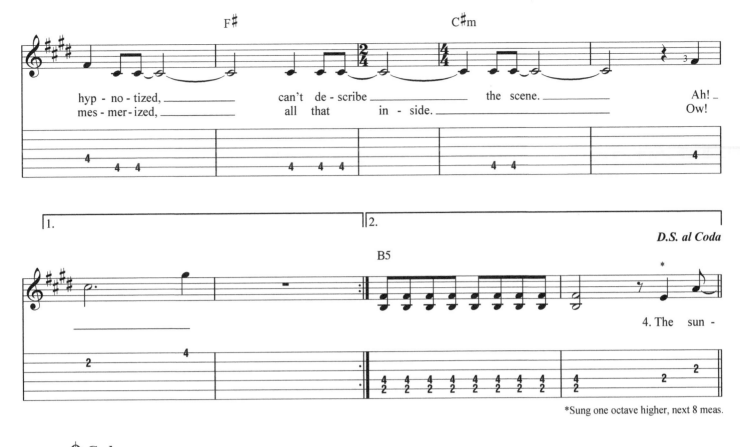

F#   C#m

hyp - no - tized, _____ can't de - scribe _____ the scene. _____ Ah! _
mes - mer - ized, _____ all that in - side. _____ Ow!

1.   2.   *D.S. al Coda*

B5

4. The sun -

*Sung one octave higher, next 8 meas.

$\oplus$ **Coda**   **Outro-Chorus**

E   B5

_ And I on - ly get _ my rocks _ off while I'm dream -

Repeat and fade

A   E

ing. I on - ly get _ my rocks _ off while I'm sleep - ing. _ And I on -

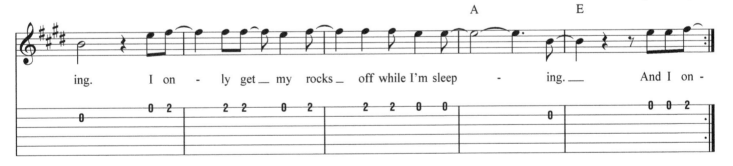

Additional Lyrics

3. I'm zipping through the days at lightning speed.
Plug in, flush out and fire the fuckin' feed.
Heading for the overload,
Splattered on the dirty road,
Kick me like you've kicked before,
I can't even feel the pain no more.

4. The sunshine bores the daylights out of me.
Chasing shadows moonlight mystery.
Heading for the overload,
Splattered on the dirty road,
Kick me like you've kicked before,
I can't even feel the pain no more.

Shattered

Words and Music by Mick Jagger and Keith Richards

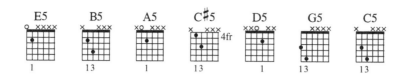

Strum Pattern: 2
Pick Pattern: 3

Intro
Moderately fast

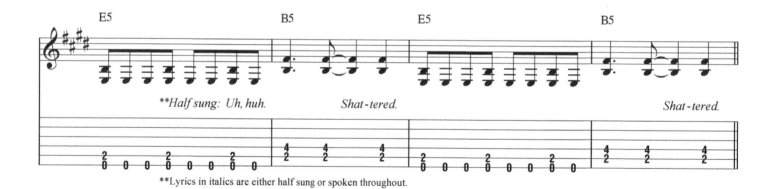

Half sung: Uh, huh.   *Shat - tered.*   *Shat - tered.*

**Lyrics in italics are either half sung or spoken throughout.

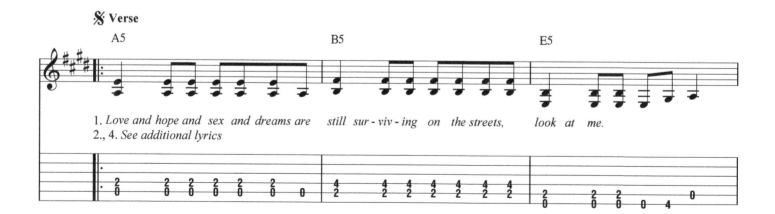

1. *Love and hope and sex and dreams are still sur - viv - ing on the streets, look at me.*
2., 4. *See additional lyrics*

I'm in tat - ters.

I've been shat - tered.

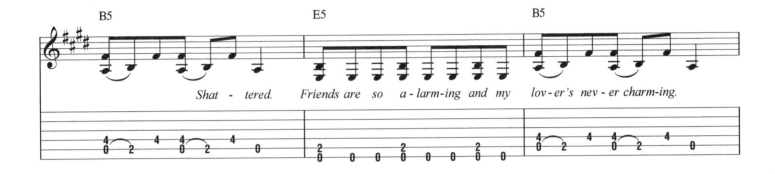

Shat - tered. Friends are so a - larm-ing and my lov-er's nev - er charm-ing.

Life's just a cock-tail par - ty on the street. Big Ap - ple peo - ple dressed in plas - tic bags,

To Coda ⊕

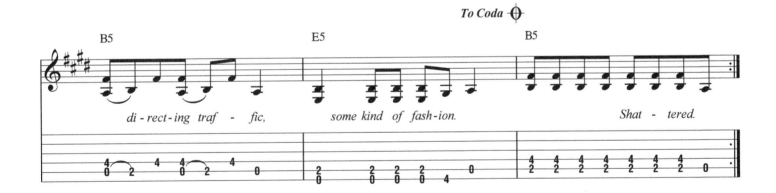

di - rect - ing traf - fic, some kind of fash-ion. Shat - tered.

Verse

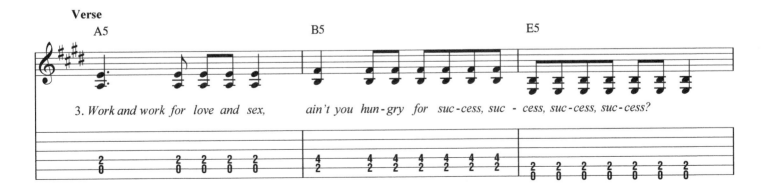

3. Work and work for love and sex, ain't you hun - gry for suc - cess, suc - cess, suc - cess, suc - cess?

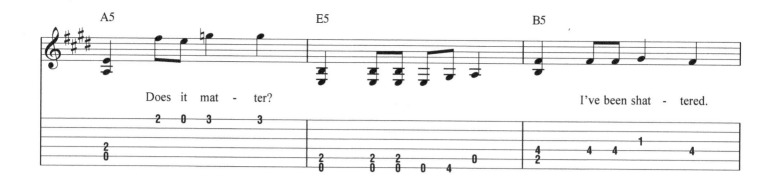

Does it mat - ter? I've been shat - tered.

Guitar Solo

Does it mat - ter? ___

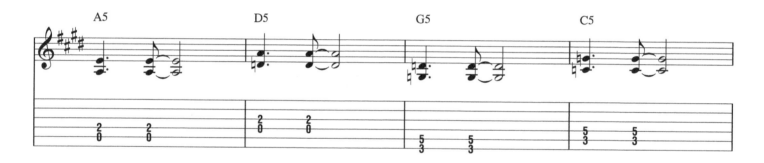

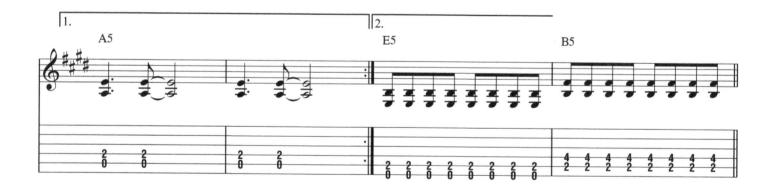

Chorus

Look at me, I'm shat - tered. ___ I'm shat - tered.

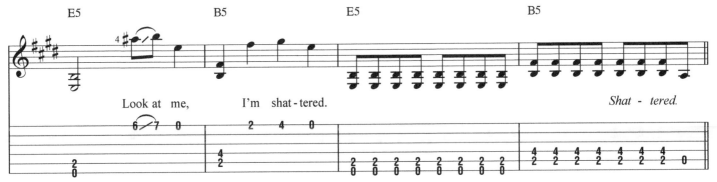

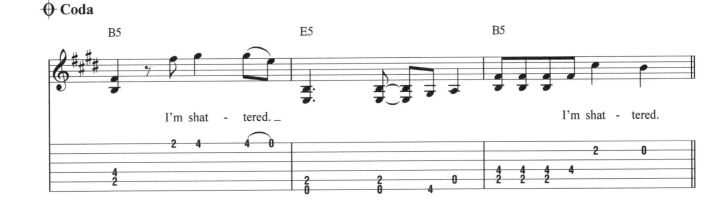

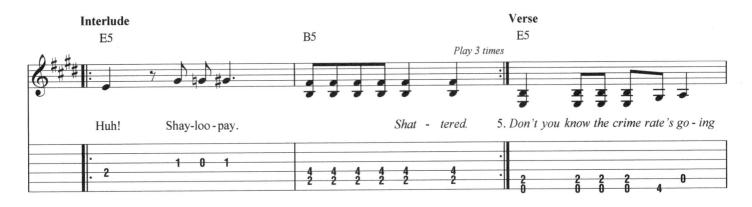

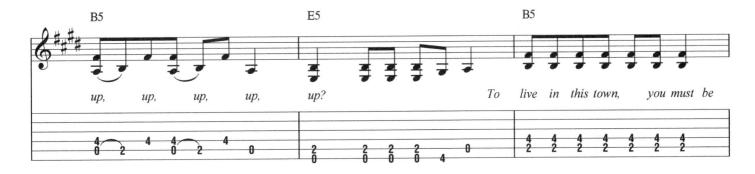

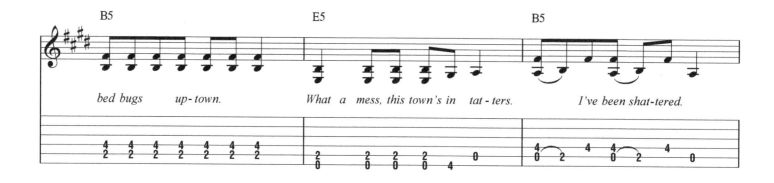

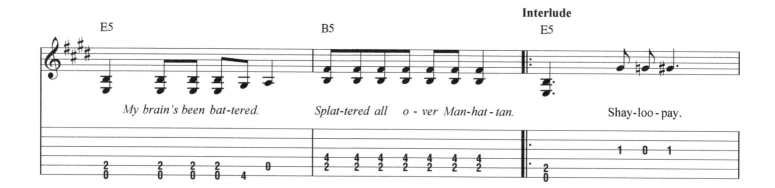

Interlude

Outro

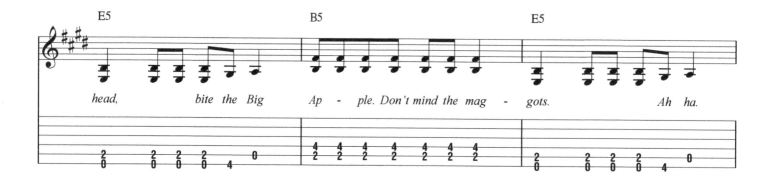

My friends, they come a-round, they flat-ter, flat-ter, flat-ter, flat-ter, flat-ter, flat-ter, flat-ter.

Pile it up. Pile it up. Pile it high on the plat - ter.

Additional Lyrics

2. Laughter, joy, and loneliness and sex and sex and sex and sex,
And look at me, I'm in tatters.
I've been shattered.
Shattered.
All this chitter-chatter, chitter-chatter, chitter-chatter 'bout
Shmat-ter, shmat-ter, shmat-ter,
I can't give it away on 7th Avenue.
This town's been wearing tatters.

4. Pride and joy and greed and sex,
That's what makes our town the best.
Pride and joy and dirty dreams and still surviving on the streets.
And look at me, I'm in tatters, yeah.
I've been battered, what does it matter?
Does it matter? Uh-huh?
Does it matter? Uh-huh?
I've been shattered.

She's So Cold

Words and Music by Mick Jagger and Keith Richards

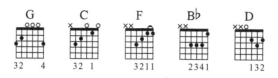

Strum Pattern: 2
Pick Pattern: 1

I'm so hot for her, I'm on fire for her, I'm so hot for her and she's so cold. _
4. *See additional lyrics*

I'm the burn-in' bush, I'm ___ the burn-in' fire, I'm ___ the bleed - in' vol - ca - no.

1., 2., 4.

I'm so hot for her, I'm so hot for her, I'm so hot for her and she's so cold. _

To Coda ⊕

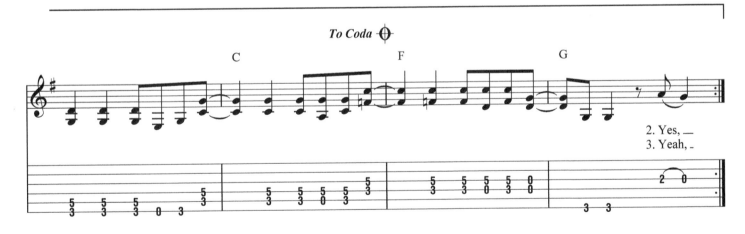

2. Yes, _
3. Yeah, _

3.

Interlude

Yeah, _ she's so cold.

D.S. al Coda
(take 4th ending)

5. Who will be - lieve _ you were a beau-ty in - deed when the

I'm so hot for you and you're so cold. ___ I'm the burn - in' bush, I'm the burn - in' fire,

I'm the bleed - in' vol - ca - no.

Outro

Repeat and fade

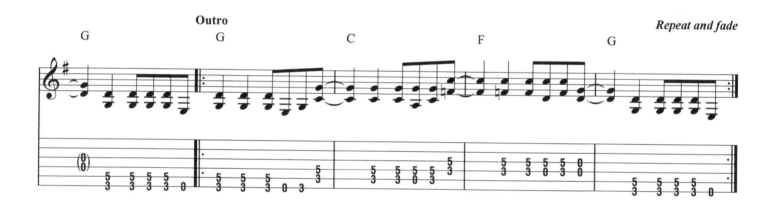

Additional Lyrics

2. Yes, I tried rewirin' her, tried refirin' her,
I think her engine is permanently stalled.
She's so cold, she's so cold.
She's so cold, cold, cold like a tombstone.
She's so cold, she's so cold.
She's so cold, cold, cold like an ice cream cone.
She's so cold, she's so cold,
When I touch her, my hand just froze.

3. Yeah, I'm so hot for her, I'm so hot for her.
I'm so hot for that queen of snow.
Put your hand on the heat, put your hand on the heat.
A come on, baby, let's go, go.
She's so cold, she's so cold, cold, she's so c-c-cold,
But she's beautiful, though.
Yeah, she's so cold.

4. She's so cold, she's so cold,
I think she was born in an arctic zone.
She's so cold, she's so cold, cold, cold,
That when I touch her, my hand just froze.
She's so cold, she's so goddamn cold,
She's so cold, cold, cold, she's so cold.

Undercover of the Night

Words and Music by Mick Jagger and Keith Richards

*Capo III

Strum Pattern: 3
Pick Pattern: 3

*Optional: To match recording, place capo at 3rd fret.

1. Hear the screams _ in Cen-tre For - ty - two,   loud e - nough _ to bust your
3., 4. *See additional lyrics*

brains out. The op-po-si-tion's tongue is cut in two.

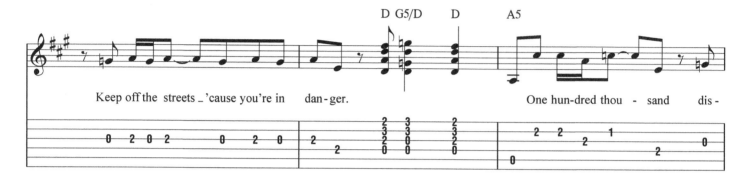

Keep off the streets _ 'cause you're in dan-ger. One hun-dred thou - sand dis-

To Coda 2

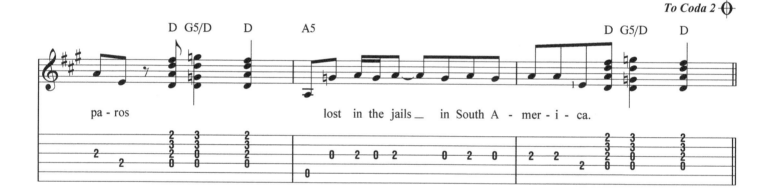

pa - ros lost in the jails _ in South A - mer - i - ca.

Chorus

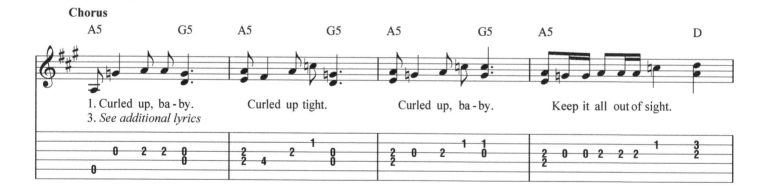

1. Curled up, ba - by. Curled up tight. Curled up, ba - by. Keep it all out of sight.
3. *See additional lyrics*

To Coda 1

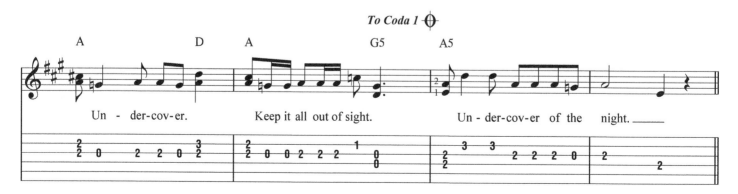

Un - der-cov-er. Keep it all out of sight. Un - der-cov-er of the night. _____

Interlude

Verse

2. The sex po - lice are out there on the streets. Make sure the pass laws are not

bro - ken. The race mi - li - tia has got itch - y fin - gers

Chorus

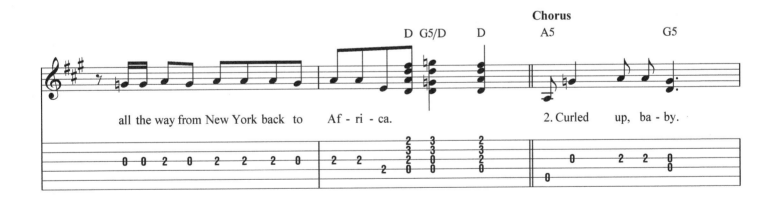

all the way from New York back to Af - ri - ca. 2. Curled up, ba - by.

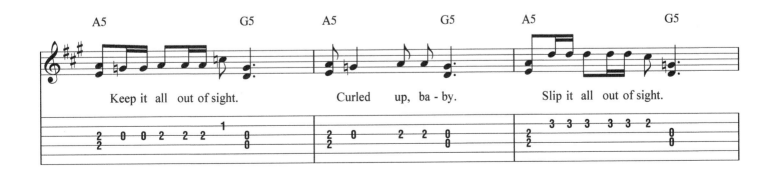

Keep it all out of sight. Curled up, ba - by. Slip it all out of sight.

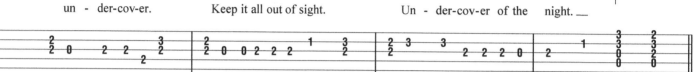

Interlude

D.S. al Coda 1

⊕ **Coda 1**

Guitar Solo

Oo, oo, oo, oo, oo, — oo, oo,

Play 5 times

1., 2.
oo, oo, oo, oo, oo.

3.
oo, oo, oo, oo, oo.

D.S. al Coda 2

Coda 2

Outro

Un - der - cov - er, keep it

out of sight.   Un - der - cov - er of the night.

Additional Lyrics

3. All the young men, they've been rounded up
   And sent to camps back in the jungle.
   And people whisper, people double-talk,
   And once proud fathers act so humble.
   All the young girls, they have got the blues.
   They're heading on back to Centre Forty-two.

Chorus 3: Keep it undercover.
   Keep it all out of sight.
   Keep it undercover.
   Keep it all out of sight.
   Undercover.
   Keep it all out of sight.
   Undercover.
   Keep it all out of sight.
   Undercover of the night.

4. Down in the bars, the girls are painted blue,
   Done up in lace, done up in rubber.
   The johns are jerky little G.I. Joes
   On R&R from Cuba and Russia.
   The smell of sex, the smell of suicide,
   All these dream things, I just can't keep inside.

Start Me Up

Words and Music by Mick Jagger and Keith Richards

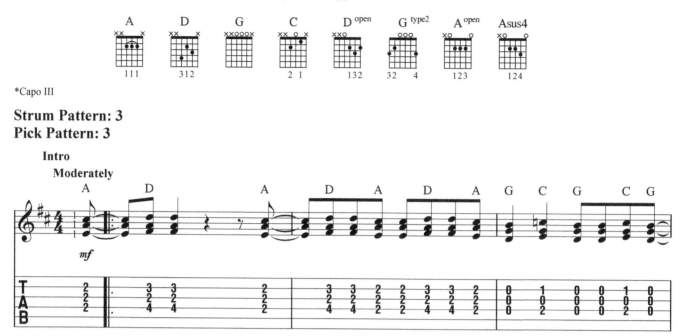

*Capo III

Strum Pattern: 3

Pick Pattern: 3

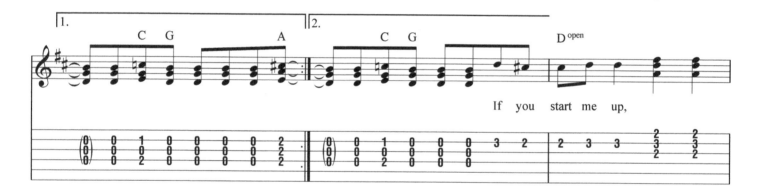

*Optional: To match recording, place capo at 3rd fret.

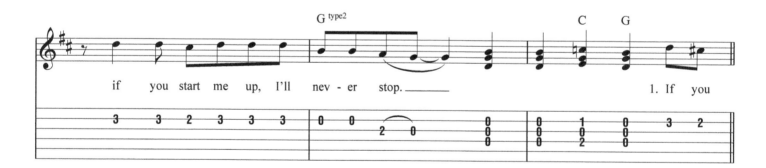

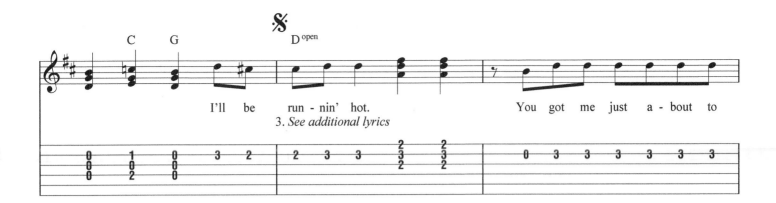

I'll be run - nin' hot.
3. See additional lyrics

You got me just a - bout to

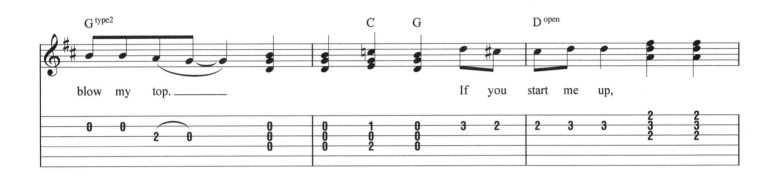

blow my top. _____

If you start me up,

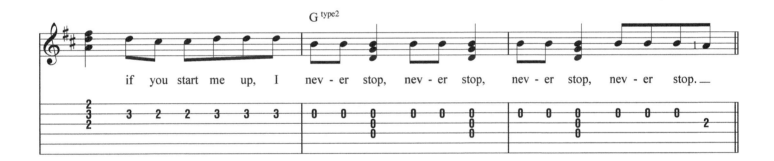

if you start me up, I nev - er stop, nev - er stop, nev - er stop, nev - er stop. _____

Chorus

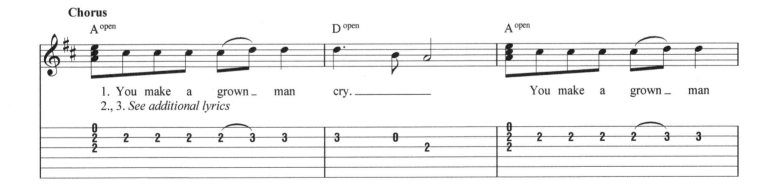

1. You make a grown _ man cry. _____
2., 3. See additional lyrics

You make a grown _ man

cry. _____

You make a grown _ man cry. _____

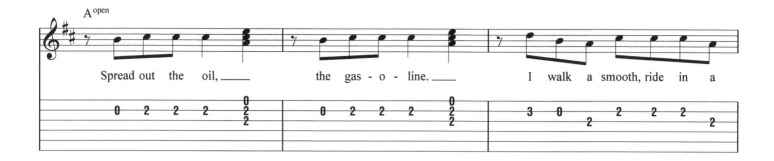

Spread out the oil, ___ the gas - o - line. ___ I walk a smooth, ride in a

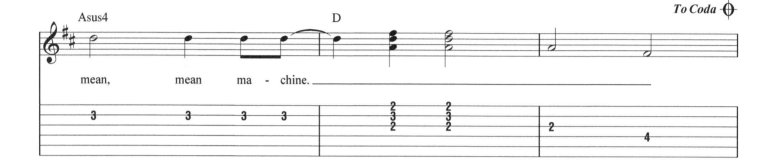

To Coda

mean, mean ma - chine. ___

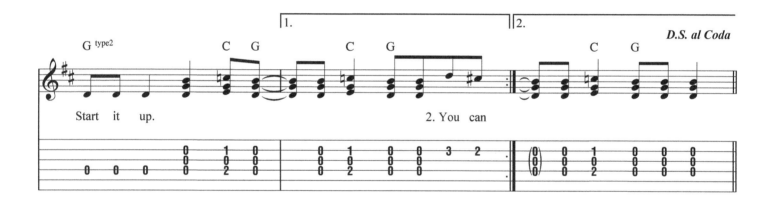

D.S. al Coda

1.

2.

Start it up. 2. You can

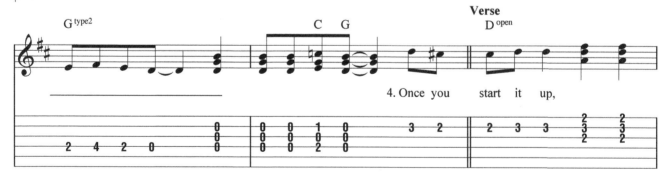

Coda

Verse

4. Once you start it up,

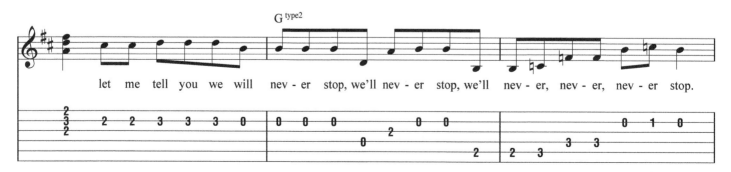

let me tell you we will nev - er stop, we'll nev - er stop, we'll nev - er, nev - er, nev - er stop.

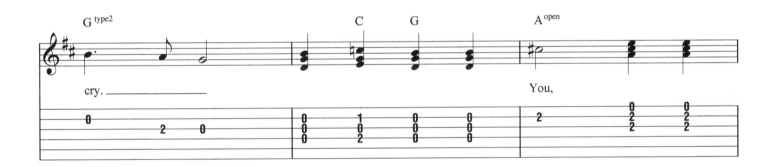

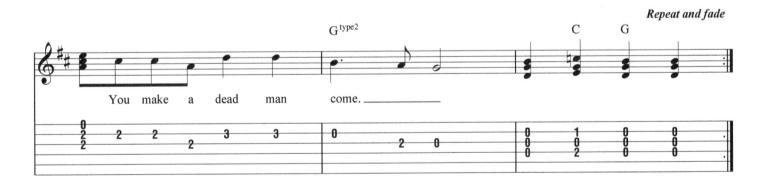

Additional Lyrics

2. You can start me up. Kick on the starter, give it all you've got, you've got, you've got.
I can't compete with the riders in the other heats.
You rough it up, if you like it, you can slide it up, slide it up, slide it up, slide it up.

Chorus 2. Don't make a grown man cry. Don't make a grown man cry.
Don't make a grown man cry. My eyes dilate, my lips go green,
My hands are greasy, she's a mean, mean machine. Start it up.

3. Start me up. Now, give it all you've got, you've got to, never, never, never stop.
Start it up. Whoo! Oh, baby, why don't ya start it up? Never, never, never.

Chorus 3. You make a grown man cry. You make a grown man cry.
You make a grown man cry. Ride like the wind at double speed,
I'll take you places that you've never, never seen.

Time Is on My Side

Words and Music by Jerry Ragovoy

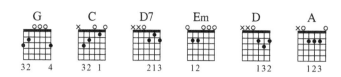

Strum Pattern: 8, 9
Pick Pattern: 8, 9

Verse
Slow, in 4

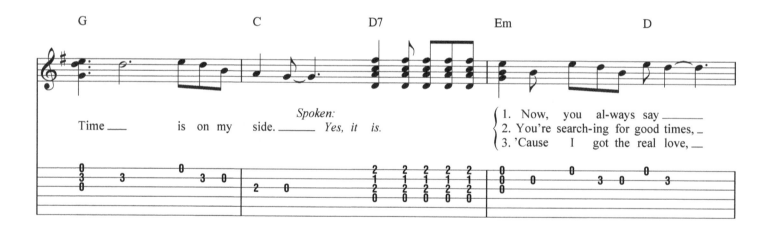

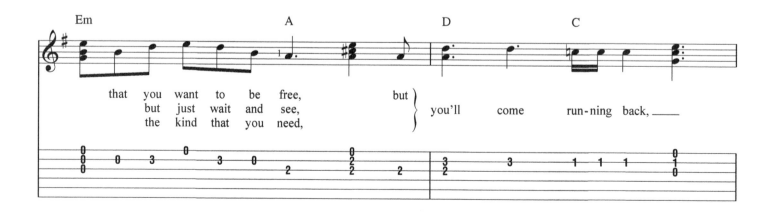

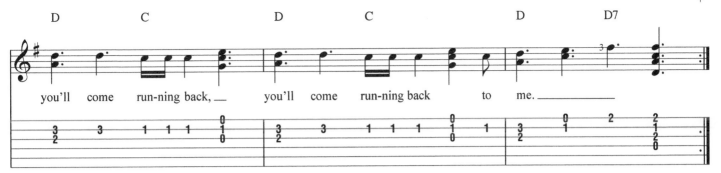

you'll come run-ning back, ___ you'll come run-ning back to me. ___

Bridge

Spoken: Go ahead,   *go ahead and light up the town.*   *Baby, do everything your heart desires.*

Remember, I'll always be around. And I know, like I told you so many times before, you're gonna come back, baby,

D.C. al Coda

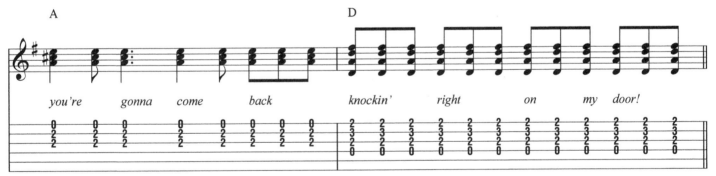

you're gonna come back knockin' right on my door!

⊕ **Coda**

Outro   *Repeat and fade*

Spoken:

Time, time, time, is on my side. ___ *Yes, it is.*

Tumbling Dice

Words and Music by Mick Jagger and Keith Richards

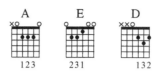

*Capo II

Strum Pattern: 6
Pick Pattern: 5

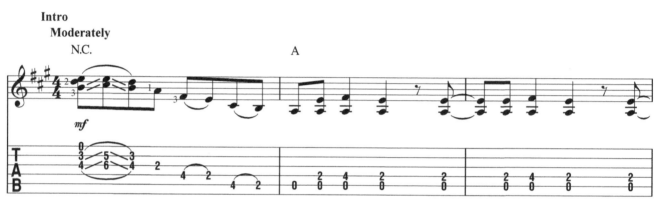

*Optional: To match recording, place capo at 2nd fret.

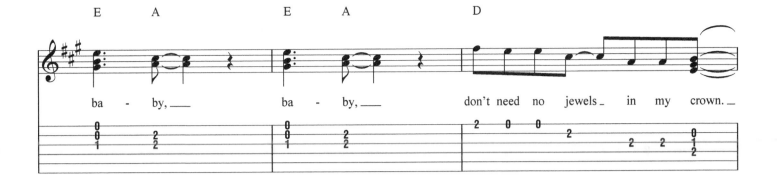

ba - by, ____ ba - by, ____ don't need no jewels __ in my crown. __

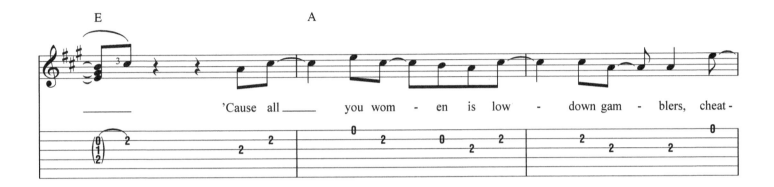

_____ 'Cause all ____ you wom - en is low - down gam - blers, cheat -

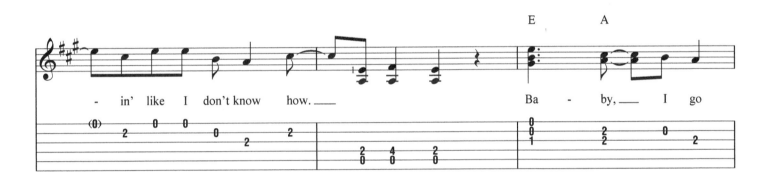

- in' like I don't know how. __ Ba - by, __ I go

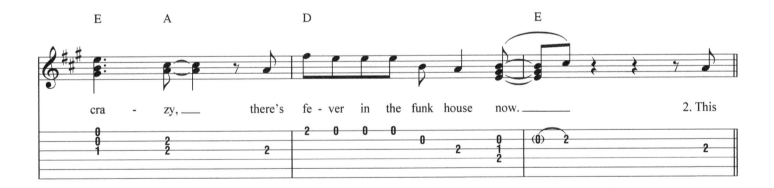

cra - zy, __ there's fe - ver in the funk house now. _____ 2. This

Verse

low-down bitch - in' got my ____ poor feet a itch - in'. You know, __ you know the deuce is still wild. __

Verse

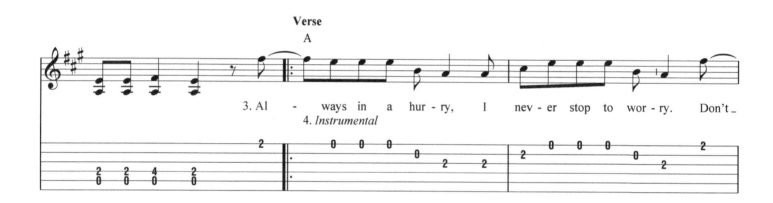

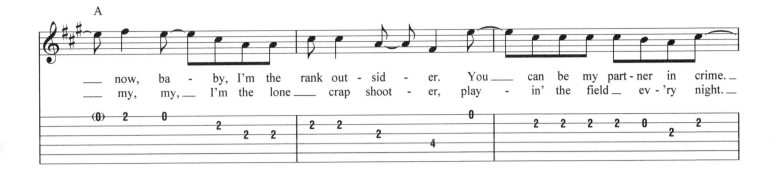

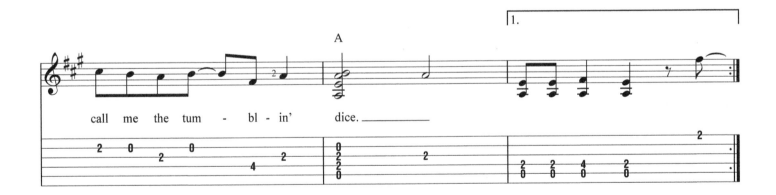

Waiting on a Friend

Words and Music by Mick Jagger and Keith Richards

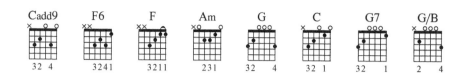

Strum Pattern: 6
Pick Pattern: 1

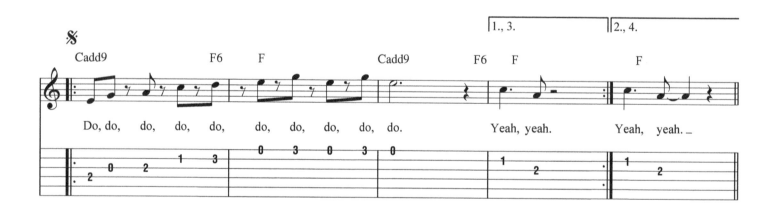

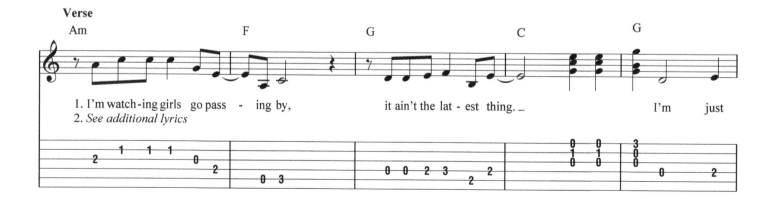

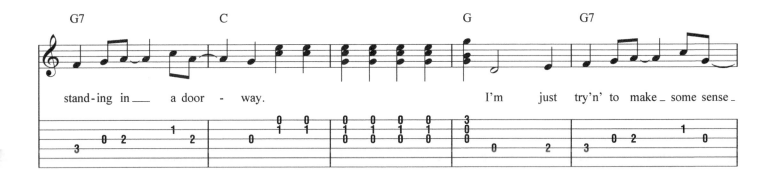

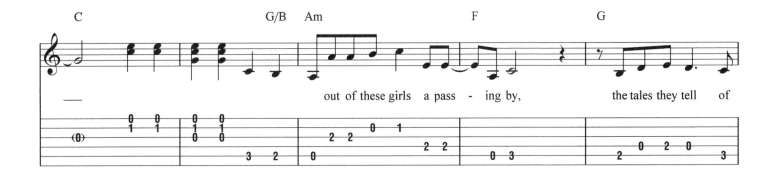

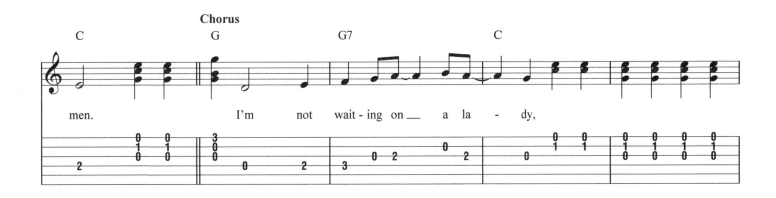

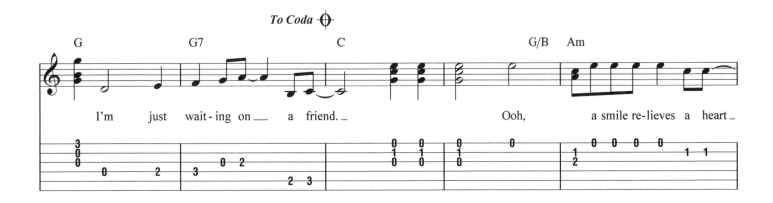

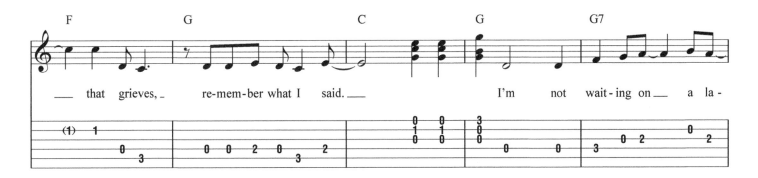

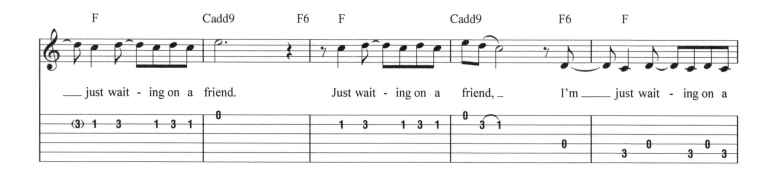

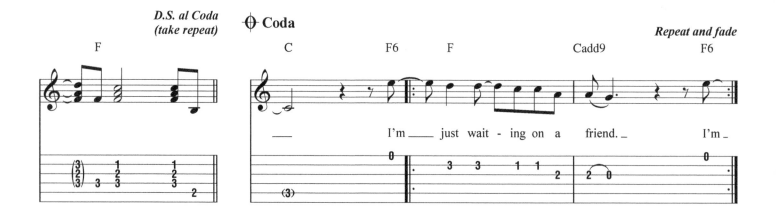

Additional Lyrics

2. Don't need a whore,
   I don't need no booze.
   Don't need a virgin priest,
   But I need someone I can cry to.
   I need someone to protect.
   Ooh, making love and breaking hearts,
   It is a game for youth.